NOTE TO P

Learning to read is an important skill for a ... ...
you can help your child reach. The American Museum of Natural History Easy
Reader program is designed to support you and your child through this process.
Developed by reading specialists, each book in the series includes carefully
selected words and sentence structures to help children advance from beginner
to intermediate to proficient readers.

Here are some tips to keep in mind as you read these books with your child:

First, preview the book together. Read the title. Then look at the cover. Ask your
child, "What is happening on the cover? What do you think this book is about?"

Next, skim through the pages of the book and look at the illustrations. This will
help your child use the illustrations to understand the story.

Then encourage your child to read. If he or she stumbles over words, try some
of these strategies:

- **use the pictures as clues**
- **point out words that are repeated**
- **sound out difficult words**
- **break up bigger words into smaller chunks**
- **use the context to lend meaning**

Finally, find out if your child understands what he or she is reading. After you
have finished reading, ask, "What happened in this book?"

Above all, understand that each child learns to read at a different rate. Make
sure to praise your young reader and provide encouragement along the way!

LEVEL 1

Introduce Your Child to Reading
Simple words and simple sentences encourage beginning readers
to sound out words.

LEVEL 2

Your Child Starts to Read
Slightly more difficult words in simple sentences help new readers
build confidence.

LEVEL 3

Your Child Reads with Help
More complex words and sentences and longer text lengths help
young readers reach reading proficiency.

LEVEL 4

Your Child Reads Alone
Practicing difficult words and sentences brings independent readers
to the next level: reading chapter books.

For Charlie and Paul

—T.F.

Photo credits

Cover/title page: © Joy Lim/Dreamstime.com
Pages 4–5: © arlindo71/iStockphoto.com; 6–7: © Dr. Morley Read/shutterstock;
8–9: © Ra'id Khalil/iStockphoto.com; 8 (inset) © Pauline S. Mills/iStockphoto.com;
10–11: © Stephen Dalton/Photoshot Holdings Ltd./Alamy; 12–13: © François Gohier/ardea.com;
14–15: © James Laurie/shutterstock; 16–17: © Pete Oxford/Minden Pictures;
18–19: © Duncan Noakes/iStockphoto.com; 20–21: © Awei/shutterstock;
22–23: © Iggy1108/iStockphoto.com; 23 (inset): © Isselee/Dreamstime.com;
24–25: © jeridu/iStockphoto.com; 26–27: © Philippe Clement/naturepl.com;
28–29: © James Benet/iStockphoto.com; 30–31: © Rewat Wannasuk/Dreamstime.com
32: © Tam Nguyen

STERLING CHILDREN'S BOOKS
New York

An Imprint of Sterling Publishing
387 Park Avenue South
New York, NY 10016

STERLING CHILDREN'S BOOKS and the distinctive Sterling Children's Books logo
are trademarks of Sterling Publishing Co., Inc.

ISBN 978-1-4027-9112-3 (hardcover)
ISBN 978-1-4027-7787-5 (paperback)

Distributed in Canada by Sterling Publishing
c/o Canadian Manda Group, 165 Dufferin Street
Toronto, Ontario, Canada M6K 3H6
Distributed in the United Kingdom by GMC Distribution Services
Castle Place, 166 High Street, Lewes, East Sussex, England BN7 1XU
Distributed in Australia by Capricorn Link (Australia) Pty. Ltd.
P.O. Box 704, Windsor, NSW 2756, Australia

For information about custom editions, special sales, and premium and corporate purchases,
please contact Sterling Special Sales at 800-805-5489 or specialsales@sterlingpublishing.com.

Printed in China
Lot #:
2 4 6 8 10 9 7 5 3
10/12

www.sterlingpublishing.com/kids

FREE ACTIVITIES & PUZZLES ONLINE AT
http://www.sterlingpublishing.com/kids/sterlingeventkits

AMERICAN MUSEUM
OF NATURAL HISTORY

EASY READERS

INSECTS IN ACTION!

Thea Feldman

STERLING CHILDREN'S BOOKS
New York

Insects are busy!

They crawl.

They fly.

They jump.

This ladybug crawls on a leaf.

Let's see some more insects in action!

Leafcutter ants carry leaves to the nest.

They carry the leaves over their backs.

They hold the leaves with their strong mouths.

A leaf weighs three times more

than an ant.

Ants are strong!

A dragonfly beats its four wings.

Two wings go up.

Two wings go down.

The dragonfly is great at flying.

It can fly in any direction!

A grasshopper jumps!

It can jump twenty times the length of its body.

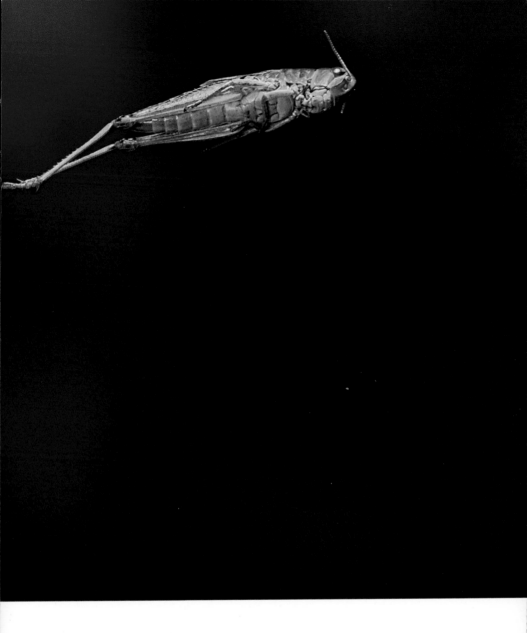

How far can you jump?

Thousands of monarch butterflies
fly south every winter.

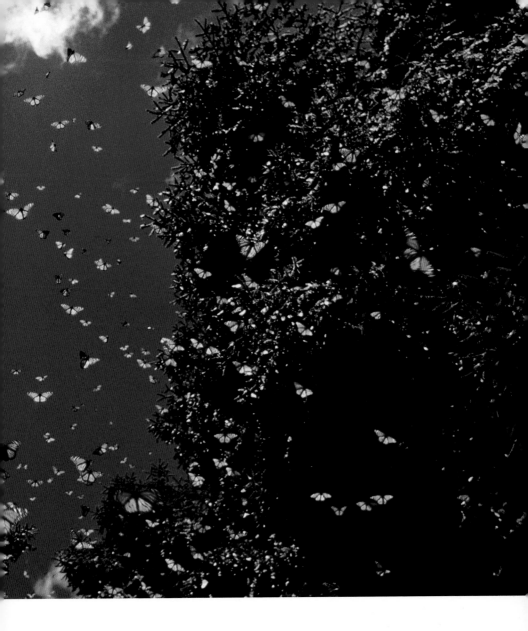

They get away from the cold weather.

An Atlas moth opens its wings.

It is the largest moth.

It has four wings.

The two front wings can reach

twelve inches across.

Hiss!

This cockroach hisses
when it gets poked.

It is a big insect.

It can be longer than your palm.

Would you want to hold one?

A dung beetle rolls the dung
of other animals into a ball.
Do you know what dung is?
Poop!

The dung beetle pushes the ball of

dung home.

Then the beetle eats it!

YUCK!

Meet the stinkbug.

It really stinks!

A stinkbug gives off a bad smell that means *stay away!*

This walkingstick is staying very still.

Can you find this insect?

It looks like part of the tree.

It stays still to stay safe.

Buzz!

A honeybee looks for flowers.

Honeybees drink sweet nectar
from flowers.

They use it to make honey.

Do you like honey?

Wasps live in nests made of paper.

Many wasps build a nest together.

The nest may be a paper home,

but it is very strong!

A praying mantis turns its head.

It can turn its head around very far.

It can even see what is behind it!

Do you see the big eyes on the

praying mantis?

They help it see things very far away.

Each insect is different.

But all insect bodies have three main

parts—head, middle, and bottom—

just like this red ant.

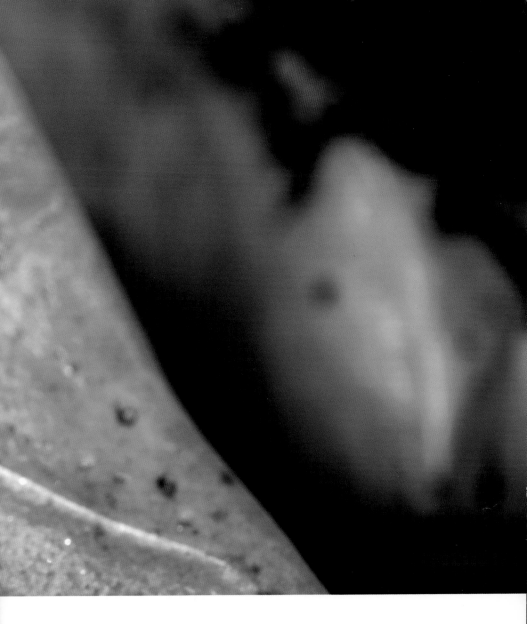

They also all have six legs and

two antennae.

What else is the same about all insects?

Insects are all busy!

MEET THE EXPERT!

My name is **Christine Johnson**, and I am an entomologist and behavioral ecologist, which means I study insects and their behaviors. I work at the American Museum of Natural History, where I help take care of the millions of insects in our collection. I also write scientific papers and teach people about insects.

My research focuses on ant behavior. I investigate how ants interact with each other: Do they fight? Do they groom each other? Do they take advantage of other ants? I am particularly interested in species of ants called slave-maker ants. Slave-maker ants trick other ant species into taking care of them. I study how the other ants defend themselves from the slave-maker ants.

As you can see from this book, all insects are incredible creatures. There are so many different kinds—from ladybugs to moths, from stinkbugs to butterflies. Some insects are so tiny you need a microscope to see them. Other insects are big enough to see with just your own eyes. Some insects are blind and use their antennae to find their way around, and some insects have big eyes and can see you—or a predator—from far away. Insects live in the hot, dry desert, in the warm tropical rain forest, on the tops of mountains, and in the water. The best part of my job is finding different insects from around the world, seeing what they look like, and discovering how they live!